All About Fish Tanks

Beginning Knowledge for the Wondrous Aquarium

Jon P Fox

Disclaimer: The author of "All About Fish Tanks" and any or all of its associates are not responsible for the use of the information found in this book. The user of the information found throughout the following chapters of this book is completely responsible for their own actions no matter what they do with it. The efforts are made to make clear any dangers of owning a fish tank and how to be safe with it; however, if any owner of this book should have issues or difficulties, damages or injuries of any kind it is not the responsibility of this book or its authors and you agree to that statement and this disclaimer at the point of purchase.

Thank You for understanding.

All About
FISH TANKS

BEGINNING KNOWLEDGE FOR
A WONDROUS AQUARIUM

JON P FOX

CONTENTS

Join the Mailing list for insider information, bonuses and gifts!
www.jonpfox.com/

INTRODUCTION

Welcome to "All About Fish Tanks, Beginning Knowledge for the Wondrous Aquarium. No matter if this is you first look at the possibility of getting a fish tank in the house or if you have one already, this book aims to bring forth answers to many of the questions that undoubtedly you will run into. It is jam packed with the pictures to help back up what is being described in the text and it has been compiled in a way that will be very fun to use.

This will be a great reference book starting with the general outlook on fish tanks and how they are made, the differences between the aquarium and the terrarium and whether or not you would go with a fresh water or salt water system. If you ever wondered about what would happen if you put certain fish with other certain creatures into the same tank, this guide should be able to shed some light on that as well. Since the fish are considered pets and the tank is intended to be very beautiful in the home you would have to understand how to maintain and keep that beauty day after day.

These days the options for a beautiful fish tank in the home are numerous and the technology like everything else, continues to expand. The scope of the book is to point you to the type of tank that you aim to have and hopefully guide you to setting up your new aquatic environment complete with the filtration system it needs. This book gives you the insight and understanding of the successful aquarium and explores the different types. With these references you should be able to settle on the size of tank and style of tank that best suits what you envisioned on having. Everything from a little bowl with one little gold fish to a massive built-in tropical aquatic environment, you will find out how experts keep these fish tanks thriving and how they continue to keep them looking great. Not to mention if you would like to possibly breed some fish of your own.

So let's jump into the book and get to know what there is to know about the world of domestic fish for the home and the tanks and equipment which is used to support these little and big guys whom which you will be calling your pets!

1 GENERAL FISH TANK INFORMATION

Welcome to the wonderful world of fish keeping! Now that you have decided that you will be keeping fish as pets, you may be thinking that it is as easy as going to the pet store and buying your new fishy friends. Unfortunately it is not that simple, there happens to be much more to it than that. But don't worry, it's not that hard either. You just need to know about the basics of fish keeping and you will not have a problem getting your new hobby started.

First, you need to learn about where you will be keeping your new fish and the fish tank. Many choices to make but you may need to start with the tank size. You will be creating an environment for your new friends to live in that will sustain their lives and I know that you would like to have the best possible home for them so just  look around the house and choose where it will be okay to put the new tank.

What does it do?

Most people think that a fish tank is just a see-through box that holds water, but that is not all it does. Besides holding the water, fish tanks also have other functions. There's the water pump and filter system, which makes sure that the water is constantly flowing and free of dirt and other nasty particles. If you use a fish tank without a pump and filter, the water will turn into a murky mess, which will not be good for your fishes.

As was already mentioned, fish tanks also serve as an artificial environment for your pet fish. This means you need to make sure that the tank is similar to their natural home, the place that all fishes come from originally. There should be sand and pebbles at the bottom (this will actually help the fish digest their food) and a couple of plants that will serve as hiding places, and some plants can even be food for the fishes. By putting these things in the tank with the fish, you are making them feel at home because you are making it look like a home to them.

This will make the fish relax and live happy instead of living in fear of their new home.

What size aquarium will you need?

Aquariums come in different sizes, starting from the small fishbowls to the huge tanks that can even fit a couple of sharks. When choosing the size of your first fish tank, you need to keep two things in mind:

The amount of space available at your home, and the types of fish you are thinking about getting. A tiny fish bowl has room enough for only one small fish! But that would keep him from being able to have a buddy. :(

You will find different basic starter fish to choose from at your local pet store.

If you don't have that much free space then you should consider getting a small tank, something that can hold around 5 gallons of water should be fine. If you are going with a small tank then you should choose fish that do not require that much room to grow. Guppies, tetras, or angelfish are good choices for small tanks (you will learn more about fish choices later). But, if you have enough room in your house, and you have enough money in your pockets, then you can go with a larger tank.

The largest, commercially available aquarium that you can buy can hold more than 200 gallons of water. A tank that huge is enough to house dozens of normal-sized fish and a couple of the really big ones like the African catfish, flowerhorns, arowanas, you can even keep a couple of small sharks if you'd like.

2 AQUARIUMS VS. TERRARIUMS

Are terrariums just aquariums without water? Many people automatically think that is the case, but there is much more to it. There happens to be important differences that you should be aware of.

The Differences Between Aquariums and Terrariums

The main difference, between these two pet habitats is that terrariums may or may not contain a certain amount of water, while an aquarium is always full to the brim.

Yes, there are terrariums that have a certain amount of water, like the ones used for keeping small turtles and other small marine reptiles. On the other hand, you will never find an aquarium that is not full of water. That is why it is called an *aquarium*, it is and always will be full of "*aqua*" which means "*water*". Compare that to the *terrarium* which will always be a place of "*terrain*" which means an *area of land* or a tract of land. You would put a pond of water to complete the terrain's surroundings.

Another key difference between these two pet habitats is this: Aquarium tanks or fish tanks, are tougher and made from materials that are more durable. Terrariums are set up only for keeping your pets from escaping, aquariums on the other hand have to be strong enough to hold a huge amount of water. They are always built to be leak-proof for obvious reasons. (Got to keep the aqua in there!) :)

How Can You Tell Them Apart?

It's actually hard to tell if a tank is built to be an aquarium or a terrarium just by looking at it, mainly because they look similar.

But if you try lifting them, you will feel how different they really are. If the tank feels heavy and the material used to make it seems thick then you can almost always be sure that it is an aquarium. If the tank seems light then it is most likely built for use as a terrarium. But always check with the seller to make sure what it is made to do before you take it home.

Around ten years ago, almost all aquariums were made out of thick, tempered glass. The problem with using glass is the fact that they are extremely heavy and it is prone to cracking or shattering into pieces.

These days, many aquarium makers use clear acrylic for making fish tanks. Not only is acrylic much lighter than glass, it is easier to form, and it is a whole lot tougher too. It will take a strong hit to even make dent on the surface of the acrylic. But there could be some dimming or loss of clarity that can develop in the acrylic over time and use, (dinged effect) which can be seen as a downfall of not using glass.

Is It Okay to Use A Terrarium In Place of an Aquarium?

No, don't use a terrarium as a fish tank, especially if the tank was designed specifically for use as a terrarium. However, you can use an old aquarium as a terrarium if you need to, just not the other way around. Terrariums and aquariums may look similar to each other, but their uses are very different. You need to be careful when choosing your first tank, do not make the mistake of getting a terrarium and then filling it with water later at home, it will most likely end up to be a disaster if you do

3 FRESHWATER AND SALTWATER AQUARIUMS

Now that you have some idea about aquariums, what they are specifically and how they work, the next part is to decide whether you want a freshwater or saltwater aquarium. This can be a tough choice because both types have their own pros and cons; you need to compare both types and come up with your own decision.

Comparing Both Types

Freshwater Aquariums

The biggest advantage of freshwater tanks is that they require less maintenance as compared to saltwater tanks. You just need to make sure that you use clean water and that you change the filter regularly to prevent the water from getting dark and murky. You can even use water straight from the tap to fill your aquarium – that is, if your tap water does not contain chlorine. If your city chlorinates the water supply, as most city governments do, you just need to put a couple of drops of de-chlorinating solution into the tank water an hour or so before you put in your fish. Although chlorine keeps the water safe and clean, it won't matter that you removed it as long as the filter and it's pump stays running .

Freshwater fish are tough, they are hardier than their saltwater cousins, and they do not require too much attention to keep them happy. You just have to make sure that you feed them correctly and clean their tanks regularly. You really do not have to monitor things like the temperature of the water and other things of that nature; however, you do need to keep the water reasonably warm if you are going to be keeping a tank full of tropical fish.

It is also a whole lot cheaper to start a freshwater aquarium than a saltwater one. The fish are cheaper (unless of course they are of a family of exotic fish), you can just use river rocks and pebbles for decoration, and you do not have to buy the water you need to put in it, but having said that; you may need to make sure your water bill at the house was paid. :)

Saltwater Aquariums

The reason most people like saltwater aquariums is that the fishes have vibrant colors and come in interesting shapes and sizes. Have you seen the movie Finding Nemo? Do you still remember the tank where the dentist kept Nemo and his friends? That was actually a saltwater setup.

Besides the fish, the decorations that you can put in your saltwater aquarium are also eye-catching. You can place different colors of corals, seaweed, and even live anemones which are creatures with tentacles that attach themselves to the coral or rock, so your fish can feel right at home in your tank. Although some anemones can be venomous and deadly to your fish, so you would be careful to not include those types in the saltwater tank.

The problem with saltwater tanks is they are quite high maintenance. You have to monitor the temperature, salinity, (salt level) and pH levels of the water, because beautiful as they are, saltwater fish are quite fragile. If the salt level in the water is either lower or higher than required, the fish could die. And if you want to place corals in your tank, you need to use a special kind of light which is required for those corals to live.

Another thing about saltwater aquarium setups is they are quite expensive. The colorful fishes like angelfish and chromis can cost upwards of $10 each, however you can get freshwater angelfish. But back to saltwater life: Even the corals cost a lot of money depending on the variety.

If you live in a landlocked state, you also have to buy saltwater, or buy synthetic saltwater mixes to make your own saltwater. Keep in mind that you need to keep the salt content of the water at just the right level; too much or too little salt in the water can kill all your fish.

If you are just a beginner at fish keeping, you might be someone who would want to go with a freshwater aquarium for now, maybe a modest 10 or 20-gallon tank. Once you have a bit more experience when it comes to taking care of fish, then it might be cool to change to a saltwater aquarium, or upgrade your current setup.

Of course if you do upgrade to a saltwater aquarium you would obviously want to dump all the water first and clean the tank. You could donate your existing freshwater fish or just keep that tank going and start from a new one for the saltwater upgrade. If you are going to stick with the same tank then it is just better to clean it out and start over by putting only saltwater items and creatures into a clean tank.

Taking those measures will ensure that the more expensive saltwater fish won't get sickly or ill from any residual contaminates that the old tank may have left behind. (SO basically removing possible germs from the old environment).

But again, if you are reading this book as a beginner in the world of fish keeping then first, that is awesome and you will be putting together an awesome tank. Just maybe consider starting out with the lesser difficult "freshwater" system!

4 CHOOSING MY FISH

The best part of starting an aquarium is most definitely choosing the fish. There is nothing like going to the aquarium supply store, walking through the many fish tanks they have, and choosing the fish that you will be taking home with you.

Of course, you already know that you should not put saltwater fish in a freshwater aquarium, or vice-versa, but besides that you also need to take a couple of other things into consideration. We need to look at types of fish that are compatible or friendly with each other.

Which fish play well together?

Some fish species are territorial. This means they will fight other fish if they get close. That will be quite a problem if your tank is not very large. You will find your fishes chasing each other all over the place, which can be fun to watch, but if this goes on, the more aggressive fish will chase the other ones out of the tank. Or they would pick on them and block them from eating until they lose energy and die.

Unless you can afford a huge aquarium with plenty of hiding spots, you should choose docile (very submissive) fish, and the types of fish that do well in groups. For instance; in a freshwater setting, plecos and cory cats can do quite well when mixed in with other fish.

On the other hand, African cichlids cannot coexist with most other freshwater fish (besides plecos and cory cats) because of their highly aggressive nature. The number of fish you can keep, should or will depend on the kind of fish you choose and the size of your tank.

Freshwater – The rule of thumb is you will need a gallon of water per inch of fish. Keep in mind that the fish you buy may not be full grown, and that they will increase in size as time goes on. So, if you have five fish that can grow to a length of five inches each (only the body, not the tail), then you will need a '25-gallon tank' to make sure that they are all happy.

So that is five fish in a 25 gallon tank that have grown their bodies to become five inches long in size. Now if you were to choose a couple of larger type fishes such as say..."Oscars", these guys can grow as big as the general environment from which they live. If you have only 25 gallons then you would definitely not go with more than two of them even if they are quite small when you buy them. Those types of fish will grow to a certain point once full grown and there won't be sufficient room in the tank for others.

Try out some of the smaller species found at the pet store at first and get to know your fish keeping hobby before trying things that you may find different and interesting.

Saltwater – This is a bit more complicated. Small to medium-sized species will require 10 gallons of water per four inches of their lengths. On the other hand, larger and faster-growing species of fish will require 10 gallons of water per two inches of their lengths. This means if you plan to keep a Polka-dot Grouper (which can grow to a length of 20") you will need a tank capable of holding 100 gallons of water. Keep in mind that these are just estimates, you can cram a couple more fish in the tank if you have the right fish keeping knowledge.

Or if you are developing in your knowledge enough that you can start to make determinations that you can control very well. The saltwater tank should have more oceanic type creatures in it based on the fact that they all live in a saltwater environment. Seeing as how these fish are more expensive, the trade-off may be worth it to you as you start to see how awesome some of these saltwater creatures are.

You would place coral reef and other plants that are very alive and can make your aquarium more beautiful and amazing looking. But be ready to spend a little more time with the care of the tank and be sure to test the water often for the proper PH and Salt levels.

When you shop for the living contents of your saltwater tank be sure to ask as many questions as you can right there at the pet store, because these folks are there constantly taking care to keep their product looking healthy and wonderful. They will be best able to advise as you design the perfect environment for your fish.

Remember to watch out for Anemones that you may buy, to make sure that the creatures are not harmful to the other fish that may swim up close to them. But try to make the aquarium look as much like what is found on the ocean floor as possible, I am sure you will enjoy this! :)

Now it is time to talk about the parts and extras you will need...See you in the next chapter.

5 AQUARIUM PARTS AND EXTRAS

An aquarium is not just a clear box full of fish and water; it is a thriving ecosystem. Your aquarium should provide your fish with everything they need to survive. This is why you need to provide additional parts known as aquarium accessories, so your scaly friends will enjoy themselves and live to a ripe old age.

To make things easier, we will assume that you will be getting a freshwater tank. To make sure your fishy friends will be happy in their new home, you need to get the following freshwater tank accessories:

A filter system – All of the food your fish will eat eventually goes out, and these wastes will contaminate the water. Over time the contamination will make the tank unlivable, unless you are taking the proper measures to stop that from happening. You need to install a filter system to remove the fish waste, uneaten food, and other nasty particles from the water.

"Uck!" So as long as there is a filter running and it is not clogged, your fish are free to do their happy dances.

Decorations/Plants — Adding decorations like porcelain castles, fake corals, rocks, and plants will not only make your aquarium look nice, they are also excellent hiding places for your fish. Why do your fish need places to hide? Well, for one thing, by instinct, they know that they are low in the food chain, especially the little fish. Having places to hide will give your fish a sense of security and make them more comfortable in their new environment. They were used to their environment at the store but now they are a little worried with their new home!

A Sturdy Stand — Unless you have a concrete countertop that you can set your tank on, you really need to get a suitable stand. A steel stand is best if you plan to buy a rather large aquarium, like something that can hold 20-30 gallons of water.

Keep in mind that a gallon of water weighs roughly 10 pounds, so your stand could carry more than 300 pounds of water, plus the weight from the tank and other accessories. Suitable stands are always available where the tanks are sold.

Just be sure not to place the tank on an old rickety piece of table that is falling apart! Some people are tempted to not buy the stand in order to save money but that can be very dangerous. So it is highly recommended that you get the stand that is made for it. Also there are custom made fish tank stands that look very attractive and adds to the aesthetic value (classiness) of the aquarium over-all.

Gravel/Pebbles — While putting a good amount of gravel on the bottom of your aquarium does make it look nice, it has other purposes as well. For example, if you want to plant real water plants in your aquarium then they will need a not-so-coarse substrate where they can take root.

The gravel you choose should not be so fine that fish waste could not seep through them and into the under-gravel filter (if you use one). Also, if you will be getting fish that likes to burrow under the sand then you need to choose gravel that is a bit on the fine side so your fish will not hurt themselves while burrowing.

Fish Food — Of course, you need to feed your fish, but one does not simply grab the first bag of fish food he or she sees on the pet supply store. You need to consider the needs of your fish when picking out fish food. You need to know if your fish would prefer live food like mealworms and small freshwater shrimp, or if they are fine with processed food like fish pellets and flakes.

You also need to think about the size of your fish. If you are taking care of small fish then there is no sense in giving them large fish pellets. Choose food that your fish can easily fit in their mouths.

Heater – If you live in a place that can get quite cold during certain times of the year then you will need a heater to keep the temperature of the water constant. This is especially true if you will be taking care of tropical fish, but it is a good idea to keep a cozy temperature for any of your finned friends.

Top Cover – The main purpose of putting a cover on your aquarium is to prevent your fish from jumping out of the water and onto your floor. Yes, some aquarium fish will jump out of the water, sometimes without any known reason, (maybe they want to explore the rest of the world...?) so you need to put a cover so that they will not fall to their doom. Some covers even come with built-in air pumps, lights, and other accessories.

Air Pump – If you will not be using a water pump to circulate the water in your tank, you will need to use an air pump to make sure that water in the tank will contain enough oxygen which is needed to keep fish healthy. Believe it or not these underwater creatures do require some bit of oxygen from   within   the   water.   (H2O) H=Hydrogen, O=Oxygen.

Optional

Besides the basics, you can get other optional components to make your aquarium setup a bit fancier, like: *Water Pump* – This will help keep the water moving and aerated. In addition, there are some water filtration systems that needs to use a pump to force the water through the filters.

Lights - What good is having brightly colored fish and beautiful decorations when you cannot even see them? You need lights on your aquarium so you can enjoy looking at your fish during the day and well into the night. You can also use a timer switch on the aquarium lights, so they would turn on and off at specified times of the day and night.

Also lighting is something the fish can enjoy as well, because there is a certain amount of light that they "*instinctively*" are accustomed to from their ancestral history. In general the fish like the light but they also need some darkness probably each night just like us people.

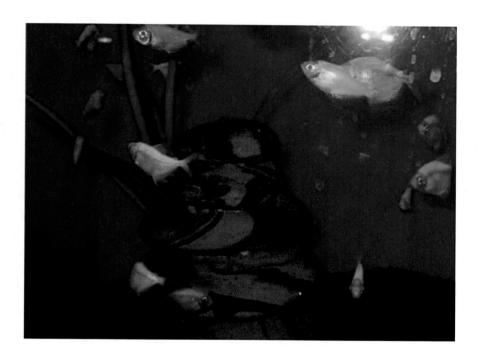

6 ALGAE EATING CREATURES

Algae are very simple plants that range from microscopic to large seaweed. They grow and thrive in wet environments, and this can be quite a problem when, not if, they start growing in your aquarium. Inevitably your beautiful tank will end up with the microscopic and the visible algae. Not only will algae make your aquarium look dark and murky, it can also make your fish sick. When you start seeing green spots growing around the corners of your fish tank you need to get rid of them immediately.

But constantly scraping the algae off the inside of your fish tank can be quite tedious, especially since algae can grow quite quickly and exists in the pebbles and stones at the bottom as well. You will find yourself cleaning your aquarium almost every day. Fortunately, you can actually get creatures that can do the cleaning for you. Here are some of the most popular algae eaters that aquarium enthusiasts keep in their tanks:

Plecos –

This is a type of catfish that feeds mainly on algae and dead plant matter, which is great because you don't have to do much housekeeping on your tank. Keep in mind though, most Plecos can grow to almost a foot in length so they are not really suited for small fish tanks, but there are some, like the *Bristle Nose Pleco*, that can only grow to a maximum of 5 inches. These fish are voracious eaters (gluttonous and greedy), so you may need to feed them with algae pellets if they have  already taken care of all the algae in your tank, if they could not find any more of the algae to eat then they will eat the other plants, so the pellets could take care of this.

Siamese Algae Eater (SAE) –

These small fish (5-6 inches fully grown), can also help you greatly with your algae problem. Besides the normal green algae types, SAE will also eat red and horsehair algae. These types of algae can actually make your fish sick; however, they tend to stop eating algae once they fully mature. It is at that stage when they also become extremely aggressive.

 These fish are quite hard to find, so if you can actually find them, get a couple of them while you can. But even if you don't come across them, it is nice to know that you always have the algae eating options. You could just keep an eye out for availability.

Cherry Shrimp – If you are out to keep your fish tank always sparkling clean, you just need to release a small swarm of cherry shrimps into the water and they will take care of that for you. Not only will these brightly-colored shrimp eat the problematic algae, they will also dispose of the uneaten bits of fish food and dead plant leaves that fall to the bottom of the tank. The only thing you need to keep in mind is that cherry shrimps are quite small so the larger fish may see them as a tempting snack. On the other hand, if you get the conditions right, the shrimp can breed and multiply.

With the help of these nifty little critters, keeping your tank algae-free will be a breeze.

So it does make the difference at the end of the day, as to whether or not the tank and all of its glory and beauty, is the result of your own hard scrubbing and pumping of its contents or if your little buddies did most of the work. Of course even with the algae eating creatures included to your fish tank there will be cause to have to maintain its cleanliness.

They simply will not be able to keep the tank 100 per cent clean. Where they will keep the glass looking shiny, they will not be able to keep the water from eventually going murky. At the bottom of the tank the waste will build-up, even with all the efforts to pump and circulate water and have to algae kept up with. So that is the time to grab a gravel pump and vacuum out as much of the waste as you can, change the filter in the main fish tank pump and then you will be looking good for quite a while after.

7 CLEANING AND FISH TANK MAINTENANCE

So we talked about the fact that even if you have algae eating creatures, you still need to give your fish tank a thorough cleaning every once in a while. Algae is just one of the things that can make a mess out of your aquarium. You also have to deal with fish waste, uneaten bits of food, and other bits of dirt and grime that will build-up over time inside your fish tank.

What will you need?

You will need a couple of basic pieces of cleaning equipment to do regular housekeeping on your aquarium. To give you an idea on what you will need, here are some of the basics:

Aquarium net – There will be some cases when you will need to take out your fish to clean your fish tank, and this is when you will need a good aquarium net.

Magnetic Cleaners – This is a nifty piece of aquarium cleaning equipment. It is a two-piece brush; you put one along the inside of the tank and the other one outside. A strong magnet will pull these two pieces together so you can scrub the inside of the tank without having to dip your hands in the water. However as we have already learned; if you are using the algae eating fish and they are doing their job just fine, a magnetic cleaner brush is probably not something that you would need on your supply list. Plecos do a great job on cleaning the side of the glass on the inside. It is good to know that these brushes exist however in case you would like to have one on hand.

Gravel Cleaner – This is like a sort of vacuum that you can use to clean the floor of your aquarium.

With this, you do not have to empty your tank whenever the amount of dirt that seeped in between the gravel gets a little too much. If you follow the instructions on how to use it, you will be able to go through the gravel and pump up all the waste particles and settlement right out of the little stones and you will notice how clean it all is when it all settles again.

Water Changer – This is a combination water hose and siphon. With a flip of a switch you can use this tool to siphon dirty water out of the tank, and another flip will allow you to refill your tank.

Sealant – After a while, the sealant that keeps the corners of the tanks together may start to deteriorate. If you let it be, your tank could begin to

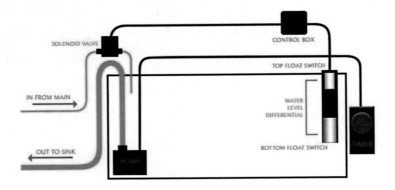

come apart at the seams, literally.

Every couple of months or so, you should inspect your tank and reapply sealant at the corners if you see that it is going away, just be careful not to blob it all over the glass.

*With these tools, and your algae-eating creatures, it will be easy for you to keep your aquarium clean. Although they add to the cost of have your new tank, they will make it a breeze to keep it in great shape and beauty. Your friends will ask you how you do it! :)

Maintenance Checklist

- Make sure that the pumps and filters are working properly, do this once a day at the very least.

- Use a thermometer to check if the water temperature is just right, do this at least once a day. If the water is too cold, check if the heater is working, adjust as needed.

- Check if the lights are working properly, do this once a day. Replace the light and/or bulb when needed.

- Make sure no wires are touching nor in the water. Unplug immediately if they are anywhere close. Use an electrical tester to find out if any of the wires are cut or damaged.

- Checklist Continued

- Check for leaks by running your hands across the seams of the tank. If you feel even a bit of moisture hit your fingers, you should reapply a bit of caulk or sealant to prevent the leak from getting worse.

FAQs about aquarium cleaning

How often do I need to change the water of your aquarium? You need to change at least 20 percent of the water in your aquarium every week. If you have the water changer tool then this is easily done. You never really need to change all of the water, unless of course something unexpected happened that made the water extremely dirty.

Do I need to replace anything? You will need to replace a couple of things at a regular basis, mainly the filters. If you are using an under-gravel filter, you need to replace it's carbon filter at least once a week. On the other hand, if you are using an external filter, you need to replace the filter media, or at least clean it, when the water flow gets significantly weaker than before. You can almost always see the build-up on that filter.

Basic Fish Tank Filter

8 CONCLUSION

Thank you again for purchasing this book!

I hope you enjoyed reading and learning with "All About Fish Tanks" It is not much seeing as how this information can be found abundantly, but it is my hope that you can find it useful and fun to have the general information all in one handy little book. A book that you can go back to over and over to guide you in the exciting field of fish-keeping. Just remember to reference this book anytime you wonder about something that has to do with your new fish tank and use it to help your friends who also have fish tanks.

Finally: If you enjoyed this book, please take the time to share your thoughts and **post a review on Amazon**. It'd be greatly appreciated! Thank you!

9 ABOUT THE AUTHOR

Born and raised in Michigan in 1962, Jon's grandparents migrated from Ireland and his parents were raised in East Detroit. Jon has an associates in applied science degree from Oklahoma State University and aspires in many different hobbies such as Art and Music along with Photography and Video. Jon has written and produced songs of the rock genre, but took a hard turn from the music business after turning down a record contract offer from a label out of Nashville, TN. Jon has changed from the music days to writing and producing product as a passion. Jon likes to stay close to God and gives thanks for the blessings in his life.

Feel free to contact Jon at: www.jonpfox.com/contact

Check out his Amazon profile here:
https://www.amazon.com/author/jonpfox

10 Next Steps

-   **Now it is time to set up your own amazing fish tank aquarium, just reference this book along the way and happy fish keeping! :)**

-   Write me an honest review about the book – I truly value your opinion and thoughts and I will incorporate them into my next book, which is already underway.

OTHER BOOKS BY THE AUTHOR

Go ahead online and type these titles into your favorite search engine of your browser to check out the other great books I've published!

Cool is the Guitar

That Awesome Place Called Space

Making Time For God

The 7 Layers of Love

Making Time For God Volume 2

Making Time For God Volume 3